D1091913

The History of a Voice

The History of a Voice

of a Voice

Jessica Jopp

SETON HALL UNIVERSITY
UNIVE...... .....RIES
SOUT..........07079

HEADMISTRESS PRESS

Copyright © 2021 by Jessica Jopp
All rights reserved.

ISBN 978-1-7358236-2-1

This book may not be reproduced, in whole or in part, including
illustrations, in any form (beyond that permitted by Sections 107
and 108 of the U.S. Copyright Law and except by reviewers for
the public press), without written permission from the publishers.

Cover art © Estate of Edith Lake Wilkinson, *Untitled* c. 1918
Cover & book design by Mary Meriam

PUBLISHER
Headmistress Press
60 Shipview Lane
Sequim, WA 98382
Telephone: 917-428-8312
Email: headmistresspress@gmail.com
Website: headmistresspress.blogspot.com

For my sisters, Jennifer Jopp and Judith Jopp

my father, Kenneth Jopp

and in memory of my mother, Madeleine Hart

Contents

I.

My Mother and I
in a Field

i.

I'll tell you how it is
when we leave the car on the side of the road
and walk far into the field

where birds lull about and gather
seeds in the August dirt. We lie down
in the dry weeds and the heat

drowses my mother into sleep.
The birds, filled with seeds and flying,
resume their murmur in the air.

When I was five,
standing in the sun-washed kitchen
with the checked linoleum warm to my feet,

I tried to imagine the place.
My mother corrected my expectations:
"We won't hear anything?" "No," she said.

"Nobody will see?" I closed my eyes.
"And we won't smell a thing?"
That's it, then. The way I'll learn to let

go of things: the birds,
having eaten fallen seeds,
fly beyond the field. All right.

But when they die they fall
back to the earth:
if we stay, keep turning seven

days and nights reflecting sun,
we are bound to be a constant
part of someone else's heaven.

ii.

As if we came like fish
through oceans of space,
past clouds as tall as ships

leaning angular and orange,
past galaxies scattered like columbine,
hung for our passing.

The summer I was eight, my father found
a cricket at the corner grocery store.
He put it in our room, for my sisters and me to hear

when fear of the thick summer dark kept us awake.
I heard the measures of my sisters' breath
rise like translucent petals, join

in sound, drift back down to cover them.
We had each other's breath
as a lullaby needed for sleep.

When the sleep being left our room
she caught their breaths
in her net of silver rainlight.

When my sisters join her
she will play their breaths back as song
so something will be familiar to them.

When they woke, drifting up through their covering
as if through shadows of petals in water,
they didn't know she had been in the room.

iii.

Before I woke, my friend and I were both in the kingdom
with our apples and our peaches wrapped in purple cloth.
And when we slid our boat out on the water

our toes were in, and the cows along the bank
got smaller as we drifted time away.
Near her temples her hair was lighter from the sun.

Now I've come here, and she has stayed beneath, in dream.
Sometimes in a voice that murmurs
like water running far below the street

she says: "I am your young one, your clock,
keeper of our days moving toward no death.
Your skinny dominion, as always."

As if we came, all voices musical, and all at ease,
knowing our transit and our brightness
beyond uncertainties, from one center moving

toward another. Knowing
we'd be dazzled by a world,
and this one.

iv.

Light sifts dust in the tower.
The bell ringer, who is young,
lies in a corner of the wooden floor.
Below him, sun pauses at every pew, breathes on.
While he dreams of a sky
iris blue, a lake,
in which he swims without arms,
the bones in the churchyard tossle.
They pluck each other and make
a choir from the trees.
And while he dreams of steel
in the shape of a coin, grief
pressing someone's eyes, a woman walks
among the stones. She puts a geranium
beside her friend. She believes
her friend can smell it.
When the bell ringer wakes the world
will be as he knew it: the tongue
that was motionless will leap.
But for now, the choir hums, the woman's grief
lives in the dust and the sun
while the bell ringer sleeps.

v.

I'll tell you what my father told me
when we sat on the front porch in the summer dark:
"Light is everything.

And you know that feeling. It gets worse with age."
All day while my father pulled weeds
sunlight fell soundlessly

on orange honeysuckle trumpets.
His bones are growing
more pronounced. What will become

of his watch and his keys?
Aging my father will lose
his flesh and his hair.

I'll say to him:
the pear tree, bursting into fruit, strewing
its blossoms, is unable to contain itself.

II.

My Father's Stone

i.

I knew 'that feeling' was the stone
I felt when I watched
the pink last rays heal together shadows

and make the whole street slow, underwater.
But underwater near the surface, where sun splinters
into fluid, and all weeds, all orange-spotted fish,

move as part of one large water body.
Everything on the street moved:
vines and trees and open window curtains

and my father's hand raising the cigarette glow
to his mouth. All without gravity, all borders changing.
I knew by 'worse' he meant more;

his stone of beauty had heavied with age,
taken up more of him. It enlarged
on less and less: a dab of sun on a chair,

sun in a drop of water. All particles of light
made the stone more difficult to convey.
Now in the summer evening air

the trumpets drop dumbly.
I clamp my hands together
like a shell for this:

for another day, another year,
don't falter under
the flower's exacting calm.

ii.

I lay in the dark and imagined
unbearable loss, wondered if poplars
in the yard would help me when it came,

or if grass or a scatter of stars.
I imagined grief had to do with words,
that it could be contained in "emptiness,"

or "Norway," or "a narrow snowy street at night
no one walked."
Here, where my friend does not wake

I live among things we have words for.
I shape letters with my lips,
and each sound, familiar, reminds me

of the death I have no language for.
Every word she does not hear, every one
says I am here and she is not.

Every word a steel bell clang
pitched high above her
soundless sleeping world.

iii.

My mother steps lightly as a sandpiper
over tall August grass of a back field,
a small scythe in her hand, two cats beside her
to clear the underbrush from some apple trees.
Her arm makes a steady sweep through the speckled shade
as she cuts tangles of weed, thorns and sumac,
and she works toward the trees over a path she has made,
piles the brush in the field, as she cuts it back.
She doesn't hum and she doesn't sing.
Her body is bent, her head hung down.
I am large than she, who brought me here in the spring,
and I lie on the earth and watch her, as we go around.
Her body is a map of scars, her short black hair
is strained with grey. Sometimes when she looks at me
her hazel eyes say: you know what you'll have to bear.
She's my mother. One hundred and three pounds, five two.
What will she be. And what. What will I do.

III.

What the Moon Is

i.

At times my mother's looped her arm through mine,
pulled me with her. "Have you seen the amaryllis?"
Then led me to it, pointed, "Look, look how beautiful,"

and I nodded to its deep orange open, blossom-mouth dumb.
Buried in the grass, I listen to my mother work
at a distance. For now it is enough to believe

in the unarticulated of this place,
in the silence with which I love, I will grieve.
The moon is a chip of Roman marble flung

up in the air by a stonecutter to dry.
Square-shouldered, he hauled it,
immaculate as bone

and dripping from the quarried ocean.
"When this piece is dry I'll make
a blue-veined snowflower, or the translucent eye

of a midnight mollie. Or I'll polish it
to be my one round perfect thing,
a monument, a weight to hold my spirit to this earth."

ii.

You might wonder
if we ran like this when we were younger,
my sister a few steps ahead,

our shirts smelling of grass,
twigs caught in our hair.
Running down Snyder Hill

our only light is the thin-milk moon-
light dabbed on trees along the road.
I want to tell her as she passes

through each age, as her body falls
further and further behind
her mind's wishes:

I am passing through those ages
behind you my body is falling.
There will be nights,

getting up for a glass of water,
when the moon, up and about,
will remind me of this.

The hardwood floor will be cold to my feet.
I'll watch the moon roll over
pulling a cover of stars.

iii.

I thought my friend's room was roofed
with winter stars, would burn against
turning. "Come sit near me," I said.

Her sleepy body came.
Then she put her head down in my lap.
"Weave your fingers through my hair," she said,

"like this," then slid her fingers through
the dark stream of her hair. "Now you."
I felt the outline of her head,

her strands of hair slip by.
She fell asleep with the valleys outside
filled with snow and galaxies.

When I lifted her head,
put it down gently on the bed,
I left without saying a word.

iv.

Or the moon is something Orpheus,
trying to distract his grief,
plucked out of the air and rolled

in his fingers. He studied
its chalky rivers,
its canyons of charcoal shadows.

He sang to it, and it held him for awhile.
But then the moon, too, became familiar.
He put the moon back to hang

in the pause of dusk,
before the stars had chiseled out their shine.
He could not look at it. He wandered.

Or the moon is another ship like the one
on which we float in the sun's slip.
From here it looks as if it's fitted out

with empty decks that echo light
and a hull that's filled with mercury or pearl.
The moon is beautiful.

Sometimes I wake to find it sailing past,
and I turn back into sleep as if I know
my hold is packed with time.

v.

And then when he was on me I thought of a bull
stomping grass into the earth.
His skin rippled wet like a hide in the rain.

I thought my bones might crack,
he was as heavy as heartache.
I wanted him to be slow

as music, quieter than the sun.
But he was running fast somewhere, or else
running away from someone.

I thought of my friend's long hair,
the brown still hair of my friend.
And then when he rolled over and slept

I watched the night move across the floor
on its way somewhere. I kept thinking
of my friend's brown quiet eyes, her long still hair.

IV.

A Dresser Key

i.

There are moments when it comes behind us huge,
a vagrant doom, huge and fine
as fever. Fine as fever when it rises
along the stem in the back of our brain,
seeps its dark blossoming along
the damp haunts. It is huge, surprises.
But when we turn to face it, turn
to look it in the eye
and watch it burn, look for the exact
place of "you must die," just then
it prisms into particulars, harmless,
the brain holds one at a time.
Particular, the angle of a pen
or the black of someone's hair,
a green lamp, or a dresser key,
fine and small and constant and bright,
says, "It can't be. It cannot be."

ii.

As we talk, brick storefronts glow
salmon in the eight o'clock August sun.
My father finishes a beer, opens another one,

standing at a gas stove frying meat.
Someone two blocks away yells that supper is done.
There are paintings of my father's

stacked beneath his bed, wrapped
in a sheet. He says,
"It was my identity. I was a painter."

While we stood at the edge of a pond
in the dark, my father explained:
"And all from one material, the content of stars,

all came blazing through the sky
like burning rain to be june bugs,
wart hogs, grass, and you and me.

It's like the spectrum—one white light
from which all colors came. Cigarette?"
The fires in our hands burned upward:

we made it safely here,
to an August night in New Hampshire.
We are what passes

between us. Stars,
we are your flung ash,
everything is here.

iii.

"It was my identity to learn
the texture of an eggshell, or of high
attic windows against a summer night sky,

to watch my hands, shadows at the turn
of the staircase where I lived, to discern
blue lines inside an onion, or the veins of a fly,

paint what I saw. I never questioned why."
Whiskey washes down the meat. He burns
holes in a napkin with his cigarette.

When our orange sparks had burned
and the air was again grey-black,
neither of us spoke, but turned

away from the sky. We looked again
to the earth. I walked beside
my father going back.

I wonder if, someday, it will fill in all
the spaces left empty. If, later,
my father will be completely stone,

completely filled and tangible,
polished, from years of movement,
from years of watching, luminous in the dark.

iv.

Bending in a stream, my friend swept
a burlap net she made
back and forth, caught heartbeats of fish
flickering in her body's shade.
The line of her arched back,
of ribs branching from her spine,
made an overturned slender hull.
She pulled movements to the surface
with her dredging sack, removed
trapped leaves, insects, and shells.
That was when it began, as if
with our bare legs grounded in the water like stems,
a June breeze moving between us fused
heat with the light in our honeycombed cells.

V.

From the Doorway

i.

The fish moves
the way my friend does
in my dreams. Slowly the stars

of color on its back
catch inside me
like swallowed spurs.

Movements
in the water fracture
lines of sun. Only they are hers.

And in my dreams her body
moves water as it goes.
Completely then, as one.

I watch her as she throws
her head back in the slow
motion of her laughter.

Her mouth moves her throat
and her dark hair follows after.
In the thickly silver

liquid of a dream
she can't hear me. She doesn't know.
And she would not remember

touching my mouth
with her fingers as I remember.
And that, five years ago.

ii.

Watching my mother move about the yard, I know
it is not her magic that draws flame
orange amaryllis blooms

from rich dirt, long green necks leaning
against the screened porch doorway of her house.
I am larger than she is now, who once was small enough

to swim, speechless, up an ancient waterway,
and picking up my heartbeat from her own,
surface through the skin-gate of her legs.

I knew nothing then of the silent
ways we love, nothing of her musk-scented clothes.
I keep learning it again. It's not the drainage sack

taped to my mother's wound, and not her loss
of weight, and not the ridge of bones
down her back, that speak for what

I can't assimilate. It's the way
she smells a peach, or holds a book,
or hears a bird, turns her head with a startled look.

iii.

We will be grand and have sea fragrances
in us, and the filtered aqua light
of the acres under

where daylight barely reaches.
Will have voyage in us, no thought of time
only of passing towers and the outlines

of buildings will grow smaller as we move.
We will be of charted stars, astronomers,
tack points on the sky map.

We will move among ghosts
and hulls, the shadowed dead.
We will be most alive.

I will think of nothing but starfish
and my lover's beautiful, urgent mouth
when we arrive.

iv.

I hear my friend walking back and forth again.
That's how I know she cannot sleep.
I think if I brought her one right thing,
one perfect, sharpened pencil, she'd be glad.
Or she would smile if I brought a stone
that had a seashell pressed in it.
But she is older. I don't know what stones
she might already have. She has secrets.
She gave me a small cloth star.
Yellow, not white, filled
and soft like a ragdoll. Sometimes at night
I roll over, and I feel it in the small
of my back. It warms me. I'd give her
anything, and anything of mine to keep,
if it would just make things all right.
Maybe if I held her she could sleep.

VI.

Turpentine

i.

Lights burned in arcs of ceiling,
empty rooms.
When I could no longer stay

in that hollow, I went outside.
The summer night sky hung
its blueprint for fire.

I stood beneath a pine,
its limbs
holding the spaces between the stars.

ii.

My father's on his knees before my windowsill.
Early March smells of mud-thaw,
of linen on a line,

smells of the moon, of a place he's never been.
"When I was young the screens were copper-wire.
What a scent they had."

His face is still, eyes closed,
and he leans against the sill,
elbows on the windowframe.

My father painted many years ago
when tones and shades of moonlight stroked his eyes,
and painting told him all he had to know.

When I was young he had a studio
that smelled of turpentine, acrylic dyes.
I watched him drink, and heard his theories grow.

He told me he loved trains and dragonflies.
I watched him drink. His hand began to slow:
a grounded bird forgetting that it flies.

Now slippery words, no longer paintings,
tell me he loves dusk, and tell me to suppose
painting told him all he had to know.

You are past change, I want to say,
as if, from somewhere far above,
someone without a name photographed my father,

before his knees got stiff,
and placed the picture among favored things:
old stars, an opened wooden box that sings.

iii.

Trying to beat her beauty out of me
I've walked to this far summer field, come where
the drowsy breath of August would agree
sometimes lovely things are hard to bear.
If I had horses' legs, could stamp the ground
to get her out, I'd beat the dirt until
there were no gestures left of hers to pound
and all the light and air in them was still.
I'd give her light and air to things
which bear them easily: the cloud-swift sky
after an August storm, her hands, bright wings
which know the way to beat the air. But I,
who do not know, must catch myself in flight,
the way a bird who dives too swiftly might.

iv.

I don't remember the passageway
where sound came to me
stretched over water.

Nor do I know if, opening with me,
my mother arched her back and released
the sounds of empty corridors.

I was only once in a world
completely hers. Now I'm in another
where no sights or tastes or smells

remind me of that place inside my mother.
This is the only way
to bring the two together: I

live without
the place where I was born,
a world from which to die.

v.

And I came, after my twenty-second year, to lie in her arms.
While far off a dark slow river ran beneath its bridges
and warehouse walls near a railyard held weathered lettering,

I came to know the smell of her hair at the end of a day.
While chimneys thrust against the constant turning,
brooms and forgotten shoes cluttered the porches

and bare bulbs streamed the backyard trees at night,
I knew the passage of my lover's hands over me.
I came to know, when the supper dishes were done,

and streetlights ghosted the darkened rooms
and telephone wires hung, the weight
of her against me held us to the earth.

I came to learn, when dark and all warped shades were drawn
over the neighborhood's errands and its gears,
to lie down with her we were widening

to absorb in our forms the heartworks of this city.
Where I'm walking the ties are overgrown
with weedy purple flowers and the ground

slopes down on one side of the railroad bed.
On the other side is a row of slanted
telephone poles I thought for a moment

I'd walked along before. But it's a photograph
that I remember, taken in 1927
where every sagging wire

along Nebraska tracks
held on in a storm.
A red-winged blackbird lands,

a peel of fire, pulls me back to the lines
I'm walking near. They hang,
as if their messages were hard to bear.

vi.

My father's passage to another place:
a wooden boat docked in a lot
cornered by Oak and Waterbury.

Between third floor papered walls he looks
inside closets, on top of and behind
shelves of peeling sketches, pens, and books.

He calls, "Where was I? Yes, Ireland, Wales …"
"Sounds good," I say, and hear his voice grow strong:
"I'll scrape and caulk the hull, and mend the sails …"

His destination is a country where
bright shafts of moon take down the sail of day
and sea winds hoist the star-tracked sheets of night,

where summer pastures roll down toward a sea
by which he came. Here he will have
twenty fields of tulips and a bay

within his view, and live on wine
from grapes hung from his windowsill,
and vegetables his garden overgrew.

His inland steps have carried him.
"Found it!" He returns, unrolls a map and stands
before the charted oceans and can see

neat fine-lined countries spread between his hands.
The whole planet is in sight, and he the North Star.
I want to say: come back, and start from where you are.

VII.

A New-World Sail

i.

I should tell you about the time
he curled up in the back and sang with beer
sloshing in his belly, his shirt front wet

with yeasty water, while our mother drove us back.
And spilling from the side of his mouth,
words like dizzied birds for his daughters:

"Adieu, kind friends, adieu, adieu."
Sun, shadows of October leaves
flashed our faces down the rippled road.

"I can no longer stay with you, stay with you."
Wandering into the yard one night
my sister and I learned

we could see a star more clearly
by looking at points around it.
We walked an inlet looking at its edges,

purple and white wild geraniums
bowing to the water to drink,
willows swooping slender arms

down in rescue,
rows of cattails swaying
above bunches of wet rushes.

We paused before a yellow clump of curled
irises with drowsy heads:
we were separate only in this world.

ii.

His wooden sailboat is soft where slugs
of August found a feast in the painted seats.
White and blue flakes have sifted down
into the lot-grass grown around the bow.
Again I've come out alone at night
to look at it, to hear my father describe
how it will look newly painted, how
the polished fittings will shine, the white
hand-stitched sail will snap.
Dogs a street or two away
bark over autumn yards
and a streetlight glows
on the empty school across the road.
I fleck paint off the outside,
brush away the cracking leaves
gathered in the corners of the seats,
as if I could uncover the exact
place where something in him died.

iii.

I learned the lines on the backs of my hands,
found rivers washed by bank lights,
tilted broadways hanging winter lamps

somewhere beautiful and distant, like Norway.
Found, while he slurred his song,
my hand a map to worlds that stay.

Next summer I will help him sand again,
paint a plank or two and fill some cracks.
I've learned to scrape the way he does:

hands, shoulders, whole body bending
into the wood, leaning into the work
for balance, none of that dream ending.

iv.

And then there was that evening coming back
from dinner when my lover and I stepped
into the darkened room, and a streetlight made black

lines across us from the windowshade.
For that moment while we stood, arms around
each other, in her eyes I saw a pause,

stilled time, or no time, and I found
words floating up in me like petals
to the surface of a pond: days,

ancient, gone, beautiful, lost.
There was a recognition in our gaze,
as if, for that moment, the effect of Lethe wore off.

v.

It's been six weeks since my mother has been outside.
She's recovering. I wrap her sweater around her
and we amble down the driveway arm in arm.

Her dusky towers of lavender guard jagged basil
and globes of chive rest in dark October soil.
The cold-slow roots of cherry trees

startled again by March will stir
each branch to hang red planets by July.
From ragged alfalfa waves across the road

white birds snap up like a new-world sail.
We hold our breath a moment watching them,
forget we came outside to get the mail.

vi.

As if my lover and I are in
a varnished wooden shell
moving over a blue canal, her hands

touch me, ease
the weight of water. We become
sun and movement. And the bank reeds,

the purple wild geranium, from a distance
sing: I want to pull
her closer to the blooming

shadowed underground. And there
where I can smell the salt
of her hair,

of the grassy inlet shoot,
a voice says: don't fear
those hands that pull

your body to the river
are also your bridge
to the absolute.

vii.

Having dreamed my hands
were dead, I sit in the dark
and watch shadows

of trees on the wall.
A streetlight did this
among other times, in 1952

in a third floor apartment
in Detroit, while the clock
on the kitchen wall

ticked the children to sleep.
In the middle of all this nothing
calls me back;

I remember I wasn't there.
I know we must have all
this time in the world.

viii.

When my lover kissed me, her mouth raised in me the voices
of women bending to a sun-splintered river,
weighted with soiled clothes.

And it raised a Spanish aria hovering
at breaking point, heard through a high single window,
the streets damp with slate-blue rain.

When she kissed me, her mouth drew from me the sigh
of a schoolgirl watching blueberries
purple a wash of milk on her spoon.

She raised from me these voices, and every one
was like a prayer in another tongue
I gathered long ago, not knowing from whom.

VIII.

A Line of Poplars

i.

That wax burned green to transparent,
changed shape in my hands, I could see.
And the vanes of the solar toy on my sill

spinning in winter light, and the copper song
of the church on the corner, I believed in.
And in the antique ring my aunt gave me,

with three small pearls in it.
I believed in maps, believed if they said
Calgary was south of London, it must be true.

And somewhere was a drawing
of fish whose eyes glowed in mercury water,
and somewhere were the fish.

I believed in the matrix of stars
above the barn, believed while straw
caught in December wind, the night sky

was made of theorems. Somewhere was a formula
for when Aldebaran appeared
above what road, in what century.

They told me my friend was dead.
I believed in the hollow inside me,
but not in what it meant.

I imagined her house, afternoon light
making shadows on the living room floor.
I imagined her coffee cup,

her watch, a print on her wall.
I would think of them, think of them,
nothing more, think of them.

ii.

My father said the moment came when he,
about fourteen, was walking the wet April ground
of Washington Park in Albany and saw
a large dark workhorse standing leisurely
before it hauled the next carriage tour around.
He realized when he watched its rhythmic jaw
grind a pull of muddy grass, the bones
beneath the brown coat fluid and exact,
its great bell-heart thudding, that since the horse
must someday die, then he would too. No magic stones
were there on which to rub away the fact,
no god to tell him otherwise. Just the coarse
straw beneath his feet, just his imagining
the barn from which the horse had come, a bit
hanging in the stab of sun that crossed
the stalls and wooden loft. Just his imagining
that was enough to wholly make of it
a place with grain and water, nothing lost.

iii.

We could call what we shared back then
the bright clear nursery of the past.
For the sake of the days our bedroom windows

yawned wide and warm October wind
snapped out linen.
A line of fine sails billowing

in the harbor of our yard
far beneath the scythe moon.
For the sake of the days we smelled

of dirt and worms, made hats of cut
grass that clumped in cool ecstatic
lumps beneath the shaded leaves,

a line of poplars standing guard
along the edges of the summer
kingdom we made: this rope

will be the moat, this stick the tower,
and this thick board we found beside the porch
will be the outside fortress wall.

iv.

Whenever we heard our mother's nightmare scream
my sisters and I leapt from our beds
and called her out of the watery silt

bottom of sleep. "Wake up," we yelled
as we ran to her room,
as we broke the fluid of her dream.

Our voices reached across a river,
each of us a dripping diver
carried her up into lamplight.

She talked her way back through
the dark figure pursuing her, back through
his hand on her mouth.

We were like guardians of Philomela,
astonished to see her tongue
quivering on the ground.

Then we talked of recipes and clothes,
our own unstartling dreams.
We laughed and joked, squealed

and hummed. We put her to bed
with loud, smacking kisses, having brought her
back to her own tongue, back to us.

v.

Heaving pines and black street wires hung
with snow bundles.
A sidewalk was marked with steel lettering

1917; a schoolyard wall had 1934
on its cornerstone; a house's oldest wing
had 1786 above the door.

It was almost two o'clock and I
thought I'd call my lover, tell her that we die.
I'd say: it is February,

I've just walked down ten frozen blocks,
I saw the chimneys and the rooflines turn,
I saw an unattended mailbox,

forgotten boots, a lost glove.
The sky a faint orange bruise
amid the black. Come back.

vi.

I should tell you first that it was in a dream
I saw bodies floating face up on a river,
eyes closed, hands folded over their stomachs,

heading downstream. From where I stood
or seemed to stand, there were
no stone towers and no steel bridges, radiant

in any light. No glints of wet grass
along the river's edge or white
and blue of cloud-life blotting the water's skin.

From where I stood, or seemed to stand,
I heard no muffled voice from the bank
or strand of song, unfaltered, filling air.

No voice except mine saying
"the living," and "the dead,"
gesturing to myself, then to the bodies.

I had to keep saying the words,
like learning the alphabet by singing it,
because things change,

and I had to keep track.
I had to be certain I knew
which was which, and the difference between the two.

vii.

Because I missed my lover
I had to walk
along the Susquehanna.

I did not have North Africa
or any other place so large
she was not in it.

Every day I followed the river
from one end of the city to the other.
I gave up the river for the tracks

of green and white Burlington Northern cars
and the rusted orange Maine
line called The Pine Tree Route.

And the thunder of the trains wouldn't do,
and not their washed-out green and red,
and not their names: Southern Pacific,

Illinois Central, Delaware and Hudson.
And not the huge blue Conrail
bins of coal rumbling south.

But a bright faceless penny
someone laid down on the rail.
I touched it with my mouth.

IX.

A Small Chipped Ring

i.

I knew there was nothing deep enough.
Not the reddest lash of petals in the room
staggered by the windows dimly lit.

They cut to the inside of my shell.
There was a place they couldn't reach.
I tried to make the purple ones cut deep,

imagined them as veins open in mid-air.
Or as fishes' bellies cut up on a wharf,
a slippery knife plunged into their pulp.

When deepness didn't work, I turned to weight,
imagined the polished doorknob of the parlor
at the bottom of a stream warbled silver.

I tried to haul it from the mud and found
it was a mass of lead I could not lift.
But even that was not like what I felt.

Nothing that was known to me would match.
I looked at the tiny wooden box
holding what had been a world to me.

I looked away. I walked
into the night longing to be,
for a time, weightless as that ash.

ii.

I watch myself write grocery lists
and fold my clothes and rearrange my books
and mark my calendar and think of a day
as a gift I am given over and over.
I watch the silver mug
burn sunlight on the morning windowsill.
I watch the magnolia in my neighbor's yard.
It gives itself away so carelessly.
I look at parts of a landscape
my friend is not here to see.
I imagine Greece
or any other place I've never been.

iii.

Since my friend's become all spirit, I'll be more
sunlight moving through thick watered vines
whose shadows lace the white walls of my room.

And I will be more fluid be more rain
wash drainpipes windows yards
abundantly the purple foxglove bed.

I'll be more pears hung bruised
with ripeness among startled white
floating from branches in a wind.

And I'll find more of her in me
in the stunned part
staring like a brush animal.

In the part of me that lies down in the yard
in an August storm saying come take me
gusts empty me and let me start again.

And since we carry our demise in us,
star particles waiting to return, she is
the part of every cell that will be ash.

iv.

I'm waiting for the breaking point
of her death in me
when I will lie down in a field

watching her blue ghost hover.
Or when I will stand emptied
of everything no longer wanting

to see her and entangle
the dark strands of our hair.
Now it comes and goes, no

clear divisions I wake and sleep
and drowse and sometimes cry
at sun or rain or pencils in a row.

The cleavings now are small
pacing in a room and saying no
no no, it cannot be

when will the quick break come.
It may never come
and I will live with her

in me past and in me now
her dying will be true but not to me
the grieving done, then never never done.

v.

Years ago I dreamed my friend died, her pink
shirt puffed around her, a magnolia bud,
carried her down the drowning river

I woke and said her name went back to sleep
now she has and I cannot sleep
or dream her into blossom dream her back

can wake, can hardly say her name
knowing a river carries her
knowing a river carries her

farther from my fingers and my eyes
what is she ash and what am I
what am I to do now what am I.

vi.

She was just walking on her summer porch
laughing in the country I remember
I wish the wind would move my curtains now

she was just here her eyes
brown and talking to me when I knew
when I knew such ease her hair

I wish the rain would come into my room
bring water from wherever she is now
coming in my window with the wind

rain wet tires over the April road
as much as these things alter time
I will join them in the altering

become seed the rain soaked yard
outside my window growing into night
and then the night wherever she is now.

vii.

The eyes outside the window
at night are wax.
I hear the bees in the barn,

cold in their cells,
thicken to freeze.
And then, beyond that,

I hear a woman in Egypt moan,
her daughter dead.
I remember the smell of her hair.

Here, in a northern country,
the sun is packed in a trunk upstairs,
or it has fallen behind a door,

rolled beneath a chair.
From time to time a star
scuttles over my carpet.

And sometimes, if I listen carefully,
the pale blue milk in the jars
on the back step hums.

viii.

The day after my friend's baby was born
I held her and looked out the hospital window.
Steam rose from a generator

and telephone wires hung and yellow leaves
minnowed to the ground. Afternoon sun
made sepia of the brick

corridors opposite,
and their windows beamed,
silver goblets underwater.

ix.

After the funeral,
when my friend and I reached The Parting Glass,
I realized my wallet had fallen from my skirt.
We went back out in the rain
and each retraced a block past
the brick warehouses again
and the parking lots of swampy dirt.
I heard him yell, and when
we met in front of the bar
he had my soggy wallet.
We went into the smoky room yelling
"We found it, we found it," and I danced
and raised my arms above my head.
Then my friend took out his money
and people looked at us, and nobody said
anything as we tossed
the bills up into the air
then ground them into the wooden floor
as if they were the tongues of the dead
or a cargo of souls Charon had lost.

x.

I will slow down for a time
when a particle moves in a kingdom
of dust on the painted windowsill.

Cities, civilizations come
then everyone goes, the empty town dusted and still.
And driven there, in summer nailed hard and fast

by steel heat of one time, one dust, one wood,
I will go down to a dry riverbed
study skulls, petroglyphs, find a way

to be of one substance unfaltering,
the dust the sun the sill for one, one time.
My tongue choked out by loss, to sing

as dust or wood or in any other form
which has a song I don't yet know
but will find somewhere, one whole and deathless thing.

xi.

She comes from my friend's womb,
from the steerage of miracle she comes here,
not a country is she from, not a sea or an island.

No blue and green geography tacked up in a bedroom
and labeled in tiny words, not the inflatable sphere
that sways from the ceiling has the point she started from.

It was dark and enclosed,
a liquid globe, with the beat
of her mother's heart everywhere. She comes

into the bright points of October sun, and leaves
her atlas and her urging behind.
She rests in my arms while the wild-eyed

cloth ponies dangle above her crib.
I rest in her breathing, having entered
again from yet another angle.

xii.

I thought her death would make me closer to things,
pain would split me wide like a purple gentian
and I'd know then the fizzled inside workings
of stars, what dies at a lake's black bottom.
I'd know why the nautilus
echoes the sea's bone beds, why its mouth
pressed to an ear, would want to speak to us.
I thought I'd know. But sometimes, since her death,
I'm farther away than I used to be
from vibrant stars and suns and backyard grass.
And the sea floor drags itself away from me,
nightshade turns aside when I pass.
Sometimes I feel like nothing. Or just a small chipped ring
dropped under a pew by a schoolgirl, forgetting everything.

xiii.

I live in a stone-floored shelter by a lake.
The berries against the window are dark red.
A deep green wooden chair stands before the fireplace.

I wake when we are turning into day
and watch the boats of summer
snap their linen in the wind.

I walk when the moon is out.
I sleep by this lake on our little earth,
steppingstone to all the light we know.

X.

I Hear an Aria

i.

Where hollyhocks issue ragged light
say purple, peach and pale red
say cloth scrap, scarf,

tiny sail, water fibered rough.
Say this time
before the wild stalk

I carry all I know of my friend.
Say this is enough.
Say this hollyhock.

ii.

The baby will learn words for things.
She'll feel them in her mouth
bright blue marbles rise

luminescent bubbles losing weight
as they go, losing color, amber
moon behind trees turning white,

a balloon someone let go.
She'll have words like "top"
for that spinning shiny flame,

and "paper" for the yellow leaves
piled at her mother's desk.
And "cloth" for the red and green

her mother weaves.
There will be things
she'll have no words for:

she'll be carried somewhere
in late March and the smell
of her mother's hair, her own smell,

will mix with dusty afternoon light
lengthening across a backyard.
She will smell the grass of summer coming.

iii.

When slants of late sun drowse me riding home
I think of a friend whose dead brother,
between bus stops at Lexington and Third,

told him not to worry, time didn't matter.
I try to hear my friend, above the rumbling,
tell me what her nameless realm is like,

what time and space and color are to her.
I want her to tell me
it was a doorway she went through

into a shadowed yard, and someone took her hand,
led her down a path. To tell me
suddenly nothing moved forward or back, but turned

in its place, which was the right one.
And red was tulip red, but richer
and blue lake blue but bolder

and green the green of beginning again.
I want her to tell me
she drank the river from her hands

and since does not remember journeying
or fatigue or homesickness or us.
Tell me she is held and rocked in ether,

that she lies, when it gets dark, against a breast,
its wet center in her mouth.
Tell me she draws from milky stars.

iv.

The baby will sit at the kitchen table
in her high wooden chair
and sunlight will purple her milk

and pieces of peach in the bowl
will change color too. Words
won't seem fluid enough.

She will look up at her mother
kneading dough for scones and she'll know
no word for how swiftly

her strong hands shape the white,
she'll know no word
for how on fire

the sharp sun makes her hair,
no word for the slope of her shoulders
as she leans her whole body into her work.

v.

After the first death whoever said
there is no other there is
there is the one again and again
the eyes of the dead
and my own voice telling me
again and again while my friend
breathed the poisoned air
of her garage, I climbed
Mount Rainier for a hundred years
or sailed to Ellis Island
from an old world and started
a new one yelling wares on Hester Street
or staked Wyoming timberland
or I washed dishes in Chicago
or walked a Maine harbor picking shells
or I dove through the pungent summer air
into an Adirondack lake, while she fell
and I tell myself again and again
whoever I was wherever I lived
I was not there.

vi.

Awake at three in the dark house I walk down
to sit at a window and look out over snow
I can't quite see. The only lights are from town

but those are far away, a faint orange glow.
And then the large amorphous shapes arrive,
dim, golden, blended with stars and trees,

out of nowhere, the whole field softly alive.
Their six outlines emerge, bulks on spindly knees.
They eat the fallen apples, shrunken, cloudy-red,

pale fires in the snow. When full, content,
each deer slowly raises its head,
dissolves among the branches.

vii.

Red tulip blazing
outside my window when I look
or do not look   blood

droplet   tent
in the desert   against nothing.
Sun   phosphorus in bones

yellow flint essential
flame from which all color
when I look or do not

look   sun fully in week
old leaf.
Eye held open   I am

look or not inside me
burns white heat of grief.
In watery green billowing

shadows of silver birch
I see again the aquamarine
of dutchman's pipe vine

leafy fish on the floor
of my friend's porch.
In purple caught in the slate

roof of the church next door
the violet of summer dusk
transparency made us visible

in her backyard talking into dark.
In charcoal grey of my room
at three in the morning I move

broken from the fluid of dreams.
I know without shape
without touch

without sight
she lingers
in this world.

viii.

For the sake of the days my sisters and I kept frogs.
We made up a whole town in the basement
with a river running through it.

We all lived on the same side of the river.
We had to swim across to get groceries
or go by rowboat. We ran a bookstore too.

For the sake of the days we would not share clothes,
would hide in the willow or in the fort,
would cry, punch holes in jars, experiment.

Then would share clothes, share compasses, keychains,
notebooks and pencil boxes. Hairbrushes and belts.
Or trade shells for rocks, rings for paintbrushes.

Would make up recipes, have teas, keep patterns,
pinned and half cut, for a rainy day project.
I kept paper scraps, my teeth, insect wings.

We walked to town for fireballs and gum.
We wore capes when it rained and walked along the moors
in the yard. We spoke in every language.

ix.

My friend has become my incandescent clot,
my exact center burning back
into the past we shared or did not.
Below the edges rough and turning black,
the half-swallowed words, or things I cannot say,
below her face floating up to me in dream,
below her shadow with me every day,
below the daily knotted seam,
phosphorescence feeds itself and thrives.
It's like the unseen center of a lake
or the axis we turn on, or a moment our lives
in their dark ephemeral glisten make
us pause, look up at the azure dome in disbelief,
no room inside for this love, this grief.

x.

I hear an aria.
The only parts I don't understand
are the words; the ascents

of sadness I recognize:
the sky is hollowed out,
the notes shaken clear.

Something was broken.
It must be
the healing I hear.

xi.

I want to tell you again,
and tell you
it was after the divorce,

whenever we heard our mother's nightmare scream
my sisters and I leapt from our beds
and called her out of the watery silt

bottom of sleep. "Wake up," we yelled
as we ran to her room,
as we broke the fluid of her dream.

Our voices reached across a river,
each of us a dripping diver
carried her up into lamplight.

She talked her way back through
the dark figure pursuing her, back through
his hand on her mouth.

We were like guardians of Philomela,
astonished to see her tongue
quivering on the ground.

Then we talked of recipes and clothes,
our own unstartling dreams.
We laughed and joked, squealed

and hummed. We put her to bed
with loud, smacking kisses, having brought her
back to her own tongue, back to us.

xii.

I imagine my friend on an aquamarine island
with netted light shaven from shells,
scattered starfish, green

ribbons in the sand, and turtle skulls.
I clean, read, write grocery lists
while she lies back in her azure world

and watches the waters stir, ages mix,
mangoes and palms growing around time's edges.
I think of her in an unmoving center

my life shuffles toward, I fold my hands for.
I speak to her, lean into
some paradise she does not talk about.

I don't mean to put her far away
in an unstartled place, where the only voice
is the shush of water in shells

dragged back into their underwater beds.
Where the music she half-hears, familiar,
is only wind running through the island marsh

tapped out on the husks of reeds,
no note human or distinct. I do not mean to.
For all I know, her island is my center,

her azure world the blue in my bones,
coal of living burned to ether
taking any form we give it.

I carry it everywhere, for all I feel.
She is in it, and we'll call it green,
call it turtle skulls, my bones, mango trees

in the medium for which they were made.
Call it my singing she sometimes hears,
water sifting sand, my heartbeat,

the wind, a hum filling in
for words I can't quite remember.
We'll call it a shadowed island

my life is grown around, and the voice
I hear inside me humming back, the shimmering
membrane where our two worlds overlap.

xiii.

It was there when I looked up from my work
to watch the carpenter hammering
a windowframe, his back to the room.

He stood on the second ladder step
leaning his sixty-two year old body
into the rectangle of afternoon sun.

And then he paused, his huge hand on his hip,
lit a cigarette, and studied what he'd done.
He ran his hand across the edge of wood

as if it were a sore spot on his neck
he rubs to ease away at five o'clock.
It was there in the bakery Thursday morning

when the heavy aproned woman moved
behind the cases with lethargic grace.
She gestured and explained

three times to me that the chocolate layered
with white stars for a border was "shadow cake."
She bent to slide the one I chose

from its tray, put it in a cardboard box. Then
she pulled some twine from a hanging canister,
wrapped it twice around and tied

the ends lightly in a bow, handed
the box to me, said "Come again."
And it was there last night when I walked

down a snowy street at nine o'clock.
An elderly woman walked ahead of me
for about a block. She wore

a crocheted hat and scarf that matched.
The shopping bag she carried at her side
pulled her body as she stepped.

I stopped to watch her turn away,
as if my look could make her passage safe.
There was no one else on the street.

Yellow light from a living room
startled the porch of a house nearby.
There were stars above its chimney,

the moon out back behind some poplar trees.
Something urged my weighted body toward
the sidewalk marked with fine steel lettering:

Hotchkiss, Binghamton, 1917.
I wondered if the aching in my knees
was something kneeling would have satisfied.

xiv.

Jupiter hangs in the high-pitched
flinted blue above
January cornfields, a lens

not close enough,
and just below the far
town lights of the dinner hour

are coming on, and streetlights loop
down the long road like lighted buoys
across a darkening harbor.

Whatever I said to damn this world
those times doubled down
from weight of love or from some lack,

whatever it was I said,
I take it back,
I take it back.

xv.

I'm drowsy, and my lover takes me by the hand
to the middle of the room where we lie
in the hum and shadows of the fan.
The heat has got us.
This is how we planned
to feel Saturday afternoon go by.
Shadows moving over land,
over lakes and fields and the sky,
in the hum and shadows of the fan,
we are falling through.
We will stay suspended
in the blue where I am drowsy,
and she takes me by the hand.
We are all we're happied by.
We will stay as long as we can.
We'll get each other water. We will sigh.
I'm drowsy, and she takes me by the hand
in the hum and shadows of the fan.

Acknowledgments

The History of a Voice is the winner of the Baxter Hathaway Prize in Poetry from *Epoch*.

Epoch: III. "What the Moon Is," V. "From the Doorway," VIII. "A Line of Poplars," and X. "I Hear an Aria"

The Greenfield Review: Section i. of "My Mother and I in a Field" and section iv. of "Turpentine"

I owe much gratitude to Dara Wier for her advice with the manuscript.

And much to Dorothy Meyer for her early encouragement, profound and enduring.

The phrase "in the country I remember" in IX. "A Small Chipped Ring," section vi., is from Trumbull Stickney's poem "Mnemosyne"

About the Author

Jessica Jopp is the recipient of the Baxter Hathaway Prize in Poetry from *Epoch*. Her work has appeared in many journals, among them *Poetry, The Progressive, The Texas Observer,* and *Seneca Review*. She teaches in the English Department at Slippery Rock University in Pennsylvania.

Headmistress Press Books

Demoted Planet - Katherine Fallon
Earlier Households - Bonnie J. Morris
The Things We Bring with Us: Travel Poems - S.G. Huerta
The Water Between Us - Gillian Ebersole
Discomfort - Sarah Caulfield
The History of a Voice - Jessica Jopp
I Wish My Father - Lesléa Newman
Tender Age - Luiza Flynn-Goodlett
Low-water's Edge - Jean A. Kingsley
Routine Bloodwork - Colleen McKee
Queer Hagiographies - Audra Puchalski
Why I Never Finished My Dissertation - Laura Foley
The Princess of Pain - Carolyn Gage & Sudie Rakusin
Seed - Janice Gould
Riding with Anne Sexton - Jen Rouse
Spoiled Meat - Nicole Santalucia
Cake - Jen Rouse
The Salt and the Song - Virginia Petrucci
mad girl's crush tweet - summer jade leavitt
Saturn coming out of its Retrograde - Briana Roldan
i am this girl - gina marie bernard
Week/End - Sarah Duncan
My Girl's Green Jacket - Mary Meriam
Nuts in Nutland - Mary Meriam & Hannah Barrett
Lovely - Lesléa Newman
Teeth & Teeth - Robin Reagler
How Distant the City - Freesia McKee
Shopgirls - Marissa Higgins
Riddle - Diane Fortney